CAN(

Tom Raworth was born in southeast London in 1938. Between 1966 and 2015 he published more than sixty books and pamphlets of poetry, prose and translations. He gave readings of his work internationally, and collaborated and performed with numerous musicians, painters and writers. His graphic work has been shown in Europe, South Africa and the United States. In 2007, in Modena, Italy, he was awarded the Antonio Delfini Prize for Lifetime Achievement. Tom Raworth died in Hove, East Sussex, in 2017.

Cancer
Tom Raworth

CARCANET
LIVES AND LETTERS

First published in Great Britain in 2025 by
Carcanet
Main Library, The University of Manchester
Oxford Road, Manchester, M13 9PP
www.carcanet.co.uk

A CIP catalogue record for this book is
available from the British Library.

ISBN 978 1 80017 462 7

Front cover drawing by Michael Myers, 1969
Back cover photo by Rob Rusk, San Francisco, c. 1976

Book design by Andrew Latimer, Carcanet
Typesetting by LiteBook Prepress Services
Printed in Great Britain by SRP Ltd, Exeter, Devon

MIX
Paper | Supporting
responsible forestry
FSC® C014540

The publisher acknowledges financial
assistance from Arts Council England.

Supported using public funding by
ARTS COUNCIL
ENGLAND

I am not suggesting alternatives – I am only pointing out where the system cut into us and hurt us.

(F. S. Flint : 'Failure')

CONTENTS

LOGBOOK

for Herbie Butterfield

Then you ask why I don't live here
Honey, how come you don't move?

(Bob Dylan : 'On the Road Again')

would have explained it. But asymptosy seems destined to leave it to Vespucci. The two styles fight even for my handwriting. Their chemicals, even, produce nothing more than wax in the ears and an amazing thirst. That seems to 'even' things, for those who regard it as a *balance*, or think the wind blows *one way*. The third day of our voyage was perilous. Multitudinous seas incarnadine. But the small craft that came out to meet us contained us and went sailing into the sunset, carrying only ten pages of my logbook (106, 291, 298, 301, 345, 356, 372, 399, 444 and 453), slightly charred by the slow still silent instant. And it was in that same instant (as everything is) that we recognised that in addition to our normal crew we had a stowaway – the author of *The Incredible Max* who, alone and unaided had, on a long string, hauled the dinghy *Automatic Writing* (out from Deus ex Machinette) – or how else could he be explained? The eloquence of his moustache (you will understand) bulged neatly over and under his belt. He spoke of himself as ceaselessly sweeping up the leaves that fall from the trees. We tried to tell him about the other seasons – 'Fall DOWN : Spring UP!' we made him repeat. 'Fall DOWN : Sweep UP!' he beepbada beep beep. Or the pages. Or the faces in the trees' silhouettes at night. Around us was the countryside of *Whimsy* where, huddled around leaping orange fires, the natives let their cigarettes dangle unlit in their mouths, thinking only petrol or butane could light them. Stripping bark from each native to reveal our track we followed one string of dulcimer notes after another. Nothing is lost, or confused, in this country – not the PENGUIN ENGLISH DICTIONARY, nor the RED PEN, nor the YELLOW PEN WITH GREEN INK (Patent Applied For). At night in the forest we slept, listening to the creak of our future oars. 'Let us,' said one of the natives whose language we could speak, but imperfectly, 'build from these trees a thing which we call a "ship" – from the wood remaining I will show you how to make "paper" – on this "paper" (once we set sail) I shall show you how to "write" (with a charred twig from the same tree) – and if your grandmother is with you, here's how we suck eggs.' From the shore we watched the 'ship' approach us. We set sail in small craft to meet the strangers, pausing only to write pages 106, 291, 298, 301, 345, 356, 372, 399, 444 and 453 of the logbook, charring a fair day. Afraid I think only in words: that is to say I am able to say 'that is one of the things we have no word for'. And when our journey takes us into the dark (en una NOche osCUra . . . roll up . . . roll up!) I am quite able, by touch, to say to myself 'this is another of the things we have no word for that I've never felt before'. And so, pausing nly to drop an 'o', flick cigarette ash into the wastepaper basket – ash which lands in the exact top right-hand corner of the only piece of paper in the basket, which I now have beside me, reading on the reverse (hidden in the basket, but the grey pattern of type through paper attracted my eyes) 'THE CHANGING CRICK-ET BAT – a clever sleight of hand trick which will mystify your audience.' – and look through the window at a man in a white suit turning the corner, I reach the end of my sentence. At the same moment the record changes. I type in time to the snare drum 'every branch blows a different way'. Ash fills my fingerprints making a soft cushing sound as I type on, pausing only this time to watch my fingers move, have a pain in my stomach, pay close attention to three words in the lyric. Now it is almost time for or, indeed, as an out-of-space static. I am writing, perhaps, the story of Atlantis: and if you can only see the peaks, and think a detailed description of *them* is sufficient, then grow gills, swim down, and get over that molecular distinction of 'the surface' and think a detailed description of an out-of-space static, or, indeed, as an out-of-space static. I am and think a detailed description of *them* is sufficient. The pen scratches on the paper, the rain taps on the window. The ship has sailed, and from inside the beer bottle we read the label in reverse through the brown glass: гиαмият. And the twig from the tree outside is stationary and dry, stuck into the neck of the same bottle. And the bottle stands on the table (the wood of which came from Finland) next to the empty cigar box ('Elaborados a Mano' in Cuba) near the Olympia typewriter (from West Germany). Until finally writing becomes the only thing that is not a petroleum by-product, or a neat capsule available without prescription. And think a detailed description of *them* is sufficient. I am writing, perhaps, the story of Atlantis, and if you can only see, then grow gills, swim down, and get over that molecular distinction of 'the surface'. Until

14

The ticket on which we saw, turning it over, the words **MAFIA MONEY** in Cooper Black type. Which meant that at that moment (the ship comes in, the craft go out – and beneath them all is Atlantis, the form of our voyage) we were thinking about Germany, and how to get there. Two scouts had been despatched to the new *Casa della Pizza* on the corner of Head Street to bring back provisions, and I was again left with the logbook. Today's happenings bear no relation to the beauty of, for instance, a brass chronometer or a sextant. But a burst of happiness comes (at the same instant as the t.v. blurts 'Cliff Richard in Scandinavia') on turning over in my papers a letter which arrived this morning from our point scout Joe. 'You're goina FIND me / out in the CUNtry' sings Cliff. The audience laughs. Do you remember the author of *The Incredible Max*? He is here too, on the telephone. But residual beams flicker 'TEEN TITANS', and the beautiful codex: 'So you girls want to do your thing in my shop? Well, let's play it by ear and see what kind of "vibes" occur.' Against which can only be set the thought of the New Band of Gypsys: Jimi Hendrix, Janis Joplin, Col. Nasser, Erich Maria Remarque and John Dos Passos. Or how do YOU think? A play with unlimited cast, each saying one line only. Or the poem that frequent deaths do not affect the bedding. Swimming around in the glass with the scent of juniper entering our lungs we screamed out. But our cries were drowned by voice-carrying laser beams which, activated by the CO_2 in our breath, boomed THE RIVER MEDWAY HAS OVERFLOWN ITS BANKS NEAR TONBRIDGE . . . THIS WOULD IMPLY THAT THE INFINITIVE WAS OVERFLY. TO OVERFLOW HAS THE PAST PARTICIPLE OVERFLOWED, NOT OVERFLOWN. The information was just in time – although in the bulb-shaped glass the pressure of the voice had forced us under the surface – for the giant finger that dipped in, stirred us around, and reascended to stroke the rim of the glass created, as it gathered speed, a perfect C sharp, which shattered our prison and caused the clear sea to overfly. How neatly all the solutions are labelled 'Paradox'! And how much we owe to Adam who never bit the apple, but rolled it along the ground, thought 'wheel', and so bought us death, clothes, and 200 different kinds of washing powder. These last few nights I wake, unable to change the film running through the two projectors behind my eyes. Of course the stars were nearer before we could fly – why else should the universe expand? And what goes on behind my head, these nights when blood splatters and snails down the shiny celluloid? Mirrors lie. This voyage can only caps. I have been from one to another of my friends and I feel uneasy. I understand now that I have been dead ever since I can remember, and that in my wife I met another corpse. This is the way salt is made. We, the salt, get put on and in things. But we are our different taste. I am in Maine. Did your salt taste different today? What did you expect this to be? I am sodium – I realise now my fear and love of water. Chlorine. We have combined to save you from our separate dangers and become the sea. Sodium rode in the bus taking care not to sweat. In front of him the strange tracery ASHTRAY. To his left SAFETY EXIT – LIFT BAR – PULL RED CORD BELOW – PUSH WINDOW OPEN. He copied this tracery as the bus sped along the dotted line. Across a pale green metal bridge. To the left grassy hillocks, then pines. In the distance a black horse cropping. He counted four blue cars, one after another. The green tinted windows of the bus announced a storm. TS 536, another blue car, overtook the bus. This is MAINE, he told himself. And the selectors threw up 'an island off the rocky coast of Maine'. An exit road curved down. A truck called HEMINGWAY passed. What strange mutations will come from that grassy strip between the lanes – never walked on, fed by fumes, cans, paper, tobacco and subtlety is only what you see looking around inside your head with a torch: beating your radar pulse there to your self and back and describing the journey. No, that was something else. Red. Until the day I (   )ed that intelligence and intuition were the same, and passed through *that* fence. The word I choose so precisely becomes next day the key word in an advertising campaign to sell a brand of stockings, because the *word* means *what comes to mind first*. And as a 'writer' and 'artist' I should have sensed the direction of that word. As the Renaissance painter should have sensed his picture on the packet around those same stockings with SIZE NINE printed across the detail which took him three days to paint. Because the stockings are always been there, and we are all USEFUL . . . and the packet was one of the things for which he painted the picture. Like the con of ecology, which has been fed and fattened to keep your mind *off*. Buy CLEAN MACHINES. So long as we are all satisfied that matter cannot be destroyed it is a closed world. 'Art' says only 'This is how I do this' – and a form can be used once only. 'He planted that word twenty years ago so that its weight is now exactly right' – that's the message of 'culture', the real, cold, science. The last message to come through on the old transmitter was ELECTRICITY WILL STOP . . . and we have no way of knowing if the last word was message or punctuation. So before

can work the transmitter we've forgotten the message.
The card retrieved from the bottle floating by said only

o
how you grow

and as we stared
a foresight appeared above the o, and it became the
muzzle of the rifle whose butt, as the picture tilted,
was cracking Rosa Luxemburg's skull. And the cir-
cle of paper from within the o fitted first neatly into
the hole of an old early morning return bus ticket,
took off, was lost for an instant in a swirl of confet-
ti, and finally settled in George Kimball's empty eye
socket as he searched in the sawdust under the table
for his glass eye. And the sawdust, the table leg, the
confetti, the bus ticket, the rifle butt, came from the
SAME TREE, whose final total of seasonal rings, said
aloud, is the name of god. On the coast of Maine
the stones are a foot in diameter. On the northern
coast of France they are an inch. Their travels tilt the
earth's axis towards another Ice Age WHICH WILL
KILL THE VEGETABLES. For this is the battle: between
the vegetables and the rocks. And we are the disput-
ed territory – we, and the water we come from and
are. And fire is the flint destroying the tree (though
it be coal – the vegetable in disguise). And mushroom
and hemp are the settlers moving west. And the

I'm not going to make it to the lift in time, nor change my name, and the dialogue echoes off the wall of the set. It's the front room, and the queen's picture flickers into a limp book called Jimi Hendrix because all books are dead, and we live where the edges overlap. The material is transparent, but the seam is already ripping down from Orion. And I am busily sweeping up the last few words in a country without an ear, whose artists are busily filling in the colours they've been allocated in the giant painting-by-numbers picture of themselves, because they think an interview with the man (now a physicist in Moscow) who was the boy on the Odessa Steps *makes a connection*. Full moon. High tide. Because it's all gesture, and nobody ever talked in words.

September – November 1970

JOURNAL

January – March 1971

January 8th, 1971

It is known now
that the best voices must vanish to the people
that any abstract could be a physical parasite
that's all i have to say today
that the path to hatred is declined i am guilty we are guilty you are guilty
that the people say 'how human that animal is' not 'how animal that
     human is'
that the purpose of education is to find why the big children hit the little
     ones – not to divide the playground by sexes and grade children
     the way intelligence, to preserve itself, does
that life is one pulse of a greater beat, suspended by intelligence
that we feel the first unsure steps of life, haltingly wearing a suit of
     intelligence
that the 90% of the brain not 'known' about is fighting back
that all is vanity (i.e. 'permitted')
that the 'unimaginable' is, because of language, imaginable
that we need to get something that isn't a thought around something that
     is not an idea
that our knowledge is as the memories of the blind

*

T.V. Bruno: 'That's not on now, is it?'

January 13th, 1971

Destroy the landscape and you create NEW PEOPLE

*

Art as lighthouse – the beam only occasionally shining on
the people on whose shore it stands. the boats that
pass.

*

Or poetry as armchair – only the basic chair, or the thing so
alien it says 'try me', is interesting. the others just
changing the upholstery or covers.

*

Get ~~the~~ those words (which are) untarnished enough *on some
facet* to reflect the light coming in from *that object*. a
dot-by-dot picture of a shape we wouldn't recognise.

*

Colchester Evening Gazette, Jan. 13th. 'There is growing
evidence, in fact, that people with manic illness
simply have too much sodium within their brain cells,
producing weird effects on their thoughts.' – strange
tie-in with page from LOGBOOK. sodium realising
that it is sodium?

January 14th, 1971

When Mickey Mouse reached Hollywood he sued Walt
Disney for calling him 'a character I invented'.

*

4,000 throats can be slit in one night by a running man –
(Star Trek)

*

A cartoon film of jewellery sparkling

*

SPEED, an historical note

> building the muscles of mind's legs
> giant steps
> it was 1956
> now here i am back again

*

Gascoyne's *The Sun at Midnight*
How sad, no, they all lead the same way

*

Art can always attract attention from intelligence

*

Familiarity of initial letter – 'E' from a blurred corner of eye
is 'Essex'

*

All art is jokes – culture preserves the ones that otherwise
would be forgotten – joke books for comedians who
couldn't be funny without them . . . and so aren't

*

coherence   is   is   thin   ~~mesh~~

        balloon   skin   holding

    in   the   air

*

a line out of formlessness

*

Dylan's 'Blowin' in the Wind' as background music to crop
    spraying on *Farming Today*

January 17th, 1971

BOOK: a ball bouncing on into the future: the travelling bombers.
    songs: 'we mean to keep hate alive'. Coat. Crisps. Bag.

*

An art that can not be made use of, least of all by the people who
    are 'cultured'

*

Not an art that can be understood because people have gone
    along that path – but a memory to be there *if they ever do*
    so they will not be lonely.

*

A TICK FOR ART must be the title of the bombing novel

*

from copy of *Tit-Bits* found on the train:

1.	Game	-PO-T
2.	Verse	PO-T--
3.	Explosion	--PO-T
4.	Placard	PO-T--
5.	Picture	P-OT-
6.	Guard	P-OT---

*

BOOK: The deaths of all Brazilian natives by 1980. 'Now trust
is dead. How many will read this speech. With one
insane from every thousand . . .'

January 19th, 1971

The people who always make decisions are those who want
to make decisions the most

*

Cells in insane asylums

January 21st, 1971

BOOK: selectivity in small matters: i.e. no dope from chinese.
'the babies in paper bags: the crippled children riding
ponies.'

*

'the idiot child smiles, seeing me there in the future watching
the screen'

*

'it depends on how many things you can trust to reflexes'

January 24th, 1971

Intelligence become reflex equals intuition

February 2nd, 1971

> the magician doesn't have any
> > tricks to show you
> white motherfuckers blues
> > boy when you're down there
> yes there's an audition
> > too, for dancing on the moon
> i'm only showing what would happen
> > if i were you

*

the lamp's reflection is orange sun on the black-and-white t.v.
moon

February 7th, 1971

INSTANT GRATIFICATION

> i hear the music in my head
> but i refuse to dance
> shades of white and grey

slam down on the drum skin
still the sky of the room i'm in
shapes that have knocked for me to play
although spread out thinly in our advance

February 8th, 1971

The Reporter's Wife: private teacher of backward rich chil-
dren: likes Cliff Richard because he's 'smart': thinks
Princess Anne 'beautiful': can't cook: thinks she's
'outrageous' because she sees her parents 'only once or
twice a fortnight' and 'lived together for a week before
we were married': dog snaps at babies: too poor to
have 'rich food like that'

*

Journalism: if you know the *truth* with what do you 'balance
the news'?

*

logic is not thin king for your self

February 13th, 1971

if the rhetoric be false should not blind you to if the rhetoric
be true

*

to be insulted is to think someone superior to your self

February 16th, 1971

mind can not kill *itself* (i.e. if glucose (?) were supplied from
      some never-ending source the mind would live on) –
      the *body* is mind's safety valve (or ejector seat)

                *

art is consciously using up pieces of dream

                *

winter light through the misted window. the milkman
      whistling, clinking bottles. a bird whistling in the
      tree. car passes. the noise of this pen. door slams
      shut in the flat below. cold. WHITE LIGHT (i.e. no
      colour of *sun* – just white on the blurred pane – pale
      green in the room) 10:05 a.m.

                *

          looking up from the works of padmasambhava
          into the sunlight i begin my will
          the trinity is obvious   all verbs
          applicable to humans are derivations
          from 'to be'   a tube outline
          traced through the air   the glow
          of an opened door. we *are*. the switching
          of relays

February 17th, 1971 (17.2.71: date reversible)

man in a london street who claims he transported london to
      andromeda out of boredom

February 18th, 1971

CLARK COOLIDGE: 'The context of these works is the tonality
of language (seen, heard, spoken, thought) itself, a
tonality that centers itself in the constant flowage
from meaning to meaning, and that sideslippage be-
tween meanings. All the books we shall perhaps never
read again form a constant background of reference
points. We are free now to delight in the Surface of
Language, a surface as deep as the distance between
(for instance) a noun (in the mind, in the dictionary)
and its object somewhere in the universe.'

February 25th, 1971

The mess has been made by men acting on their theories.
The senses pick up fuel from space for the mind to
move through time. Intuition skips language it doesn't
'know' and reappears where the words fit again.
Surgery now is headed towards mind in time. We can
be nowhere else *but* at the end (thought and memory
keeping *all* space together in time?). Poetry is am-
bergris (cast on what?) (or solidified mixture of space
and time?). Boring 'now' – using up 'time'?

*

'That time is space made fluid' (Myra Breckinridge)

*

OUR SENSES ARE AS GUIDE DOGS TO THE BLIND.   WHERE ARE
THE LAMPPOSTS?   WHERE IS THE TRAFFIC?   AND WE CANNOT
SAY EVEN 'WHAT?'

*

DNA – learning transfer by injection – ART BY PILL – mixed
media nothing new – just *using up* still-applicable
pieces. STILL remain writing (language, pen, paper)
PAINTING/SCULPTURE (moulding of anything) and
MUSIC (voice, whistle) – cassette for prose plus image.
holograms. or how about a drug to take you some-
where else while you work in impossible conditions?
overcrowding. to feel in a field while jammed in a
room.

*

Katonah, where I waited with Jim on the station in the snow,
I find now is where Apollinaire's Annie Playden
moved to and lives (lived?)

*

the beautiful life of a great poet – living second after second
among his rejected poems. they think.

*

'70s. Neil Young. The Places. The Basement. Dylan.
Weathermen. NY.

*

video cassette of film of Will Rogers roping / Tom Mix
explaining

*

UNRELATED DATA GIVE A SIGNATURE OF THE FUTURE

February 26th, 1971

JANIS JOPLIN

look at the animals we've been given as toys
sensual gestures change
with the speed of getting it
listen to the shell and
hear a cry for help from the sea
what is hysteria?
what is control?

February 28th, 1971

He hath filled the hungry w/ good things and the rich he
    hath sent hungry away?

*

events have expanded further than language can explain in
    time

March 3rd, 1971

yes, i wrestle
with my art
over my head quick
now a sneak attack
i kick poetry in the face

drums in my head
i step on
the body of my muse
look at the view
as the event balloon blows up

unless it is true
and says yes
when you look for it yes
here it is again
yes, i wrestle, what about supper?

*

How about companies paying the wages they've saved during
a strike into a central welfare fund?

March 14th, 1971

'If it's cocaine with you, it's cocaine with me.'

*

What could set time alight and burn it away?

March 15th, 1971

When you talk about it you're covered in ice. Let me tell
you it will get more abstruse and the references will
make you feel ignorant. So why did you suck that
dummy, preserving your own space? That wasn't
the instruction. To recoil from a knee or a foot and
blush. Or snug in the michelin body of your 'family'.
If the cinema film moves frame to still frame, and the
t.v. picture is shot from scanning guns, what makes
you think there is movement? Because *you* move?
Come on! Light, Time and Space. The three verbs.

March 17th, 1971 (17.3.71)

      funny thing
      blast

                    *

      i
      is a fully
      qualified neurosurgeon

      end of a letter
      a girder through rock

                    *

      light is time
      t is t

March 19th, 1971

The centre is inflatable – language had set like marzipan – events
      and populations burst it open – mistaken that language
      'contains' events. the object of art is no longer to be
      outside and to be thought about – but to put the electric
      wires into the dead dog of language and get a twitch.

March 21st, 1971

      there were traces of mind left on the
      bullet that sped through my head

      too fast for life to see

      the whole picture

the artist's mind scans for the new and is thus opposed to
the critic's which reads everything. thus the critics
kill more trees for longer books. the people of the
rock (manic . . . sodium . . . rock . . . kerouac). wind
(written on) carries the pollen (and the bees) and
thus serves vegetable (also reducing the bulk of rock)
(thus the vegetable feeds on rock dust (earth) + life).
what happens to pollen on the rocks? lichen? does
this rot the rocks? or rock making shade. trees are
cracking the planet open. the cracks that caused the
continental drift . . . and the *king doms*. body + life
+ rock = earth . . . plants. body . . . worms . . . earth
. . . plants. what a game it is! the random machine
puts up memories . . . like orange, lemon or raspberry.
what should 'life' 'think'? why should one be depen-
dent on the other? think and feel? but it could all
be done by two people . . . as a joke. stay where you're
happy. it always seems to be a choice of instructions
. . . and what happens if you reductio ad absurdum
that? so *feeling* is the key. maybe there are four forc-
es using our 'self's. all that information. all truth is
truth and you will recognise it because it's bigger than
all of us . . . i.e. . . . we can all only see a piece. (who's
doing the North Face this year?) you can't compose
. . . the truth will out . . . and why should you suppose
it is *noble*? . . . the truth is all. if I go on writing I'm
only writing for others whose opinion I 'value' . . . i.e.
they already see the same view and compliment me
on how accurate my picture is . . . or, for the *explainers*.
what lives in the shadow where the beam from art's
lighthouse is blocked by the bulk of truth? and what
is the darkness compared with which we have life?
we have now to ask ourselves what is truth hiding?

something pointing all ways must have a centre . . . or
be purely mathematical.   everything is pandering to
people's wants . . . and people's wants is every thing.

*

'i hear you're hitting people'
'one at a time'

why do you want to
remember your thoughts

you've got such a
come on it's an illness

to me

wanting the devouring
woman is its opposite

any piece of language
will fuse with any other piece

you
can't
contra
dict
your
self

any piece of language
contains *meaning*

that's what
we're fighting against

LETTERS FROM YADDO

April – May 1971

*He was, he said, just a lone monk walking the world
with a leaky umbrella*

(Edward Crankshaw : Interview with Mao)

Dear Ed: Sorry to miss you when I called, but I was happy to hear Jenny and learn you were all OK. I got here yesterday evening on the bus from New York: now it's a bright spring morning. I think I'll keep some sort of a diary . . . no . . . what I mean is I'll type out the day's events each morning and mail it to you. That way I won't have a copy here to read with hindsight. I get nervous about carbons . . . they're really secretive. So what's new? I had a card from Anselm waiting for me saying there's no job in Iowa – which I'd known for at least thirty-three years – and also that he had doubts about his own. I wrote a joke poem the day before I left Colchester, which, on rereading, seems to say all I can about England:

SONNET DAZE

i watch myself grow larger in her eyes
and clutch a yellow feather near its tip
as if to mark with ink that never dries
the yet uncharted voyage of my ship

those two flat images project and form
the looming solid that contains my mind
whilst independently the quill writes 'warm'
dreaming its tip still in the bird's behind

since those two stanzas many days have passed
now percy thrower speaks of roses on t.v.
morecambe and wise with full supporting cast
will soon be on – i call for val to see

the fire is red   the cat licks down her tail
i close my eyes and read the rest in braille

What else? Yes, Val and the kids came out to the airport with me (shit . . . why don't I just write a book and send it? . . . I mean what was I thinking of? . . . a *journal*! . . . jesus, I can see it bound in leather saying JOURNAL on the cover). OK. We're into the book. It was so easy. Just like being alive. I can't stop laughing. Right. Val and the kids came out to the airport with me, then went down to stay with her mother on the coast for a few days. That 'flu germ hung around a long time . . . and Val got it last . . . so I hope the sea air blows it away. Jenny said you were going into the country. Will you be in Chicago around May 16th/17th? I have to leave on the 18th in the afternoon.

I got worried about writing the other day. Sitting talking to someone – or rather listening to someone talking – I caught myself making mental notes of what was being said to write them up later. Not only that, but I got really irritated with the person talking because I was having to file the memory rapidly in the back of my head so I could listen to the radio to catch the name of a record that was playing and the voice was drowning it out. So I scribbled it all down as it was because I realised that's what a writer is and you can only use yourself in the most truthful way possible (by the way, this book is called AMERICA LEAVES). This is what I wrote down:

> not writing the truth. writing that. holding that in my head while i bitch to myself about the dialogue because i can't hear the name of the record. thanks, jack, although your death is as sadness in aspic in ted's poem. buying your time and space and thinking about it. the forks are character and life. take life. from the intersection silver buses shimmer towards me in the heat haze. a blue shape crosses the road. eternal rest. now you'd be interested if this were character, which reappears from the separation of character and

life. jimi hendrix castles made of sand. if this is not truth it doesn't work and how would you know? pause about your head. skyline i'm interested in. i mean the machine has limits . . . not only the people you 'happen to run into', but the basketball game. bradley and barnett. don't look . . . don't look at him. car horn from outside; crumpled paper from within. the breeze rustles all the leaves of the sweet potato plant. all grit is left in the grille. so i'm not going to sublimate it by putting it into the mouths of 'characters' . . . or/ and letting them take over. if you can't give it straight there's no point in being a radio (radio-lib stand-up!). this is a trip through the world of writing, you vicarious heads. if you want to work *that* slow here comes the cancer. and i don't want a piece of you to mature in my pouch now that tape is running through me. you know they filter it off into interviews while 'we want food' comes through in blurred waves. so let's give them content that extends to any flat edge they'd call 'form'. i scream it out through this maze of pines. i love you (all of you i love, that is). keep everyone in the world awake at the same time (alarm clocks) and we disappear

Now I'm sure I had a note a couple of days ago that ties in with that. My yellow pencil shakes with the vibration from the typewriter and I stop to read its inscription: THINK AND SUGGEST – STATE OF N.J. 550. My notebook now. No, looks like I never wrote it down. But here's all that's there:

April 1st

> very profound
> and almost round

the story of the three verbs
light   time   and space

their coast
isn't my coast

*

good evening
i am worn away by your kisses
god i was good

*

that song
that you remember

*

turning and turning and turning it is really scandalous
how we jump up and down on the international
date line. i follow the sun – and they call them the
backward nations

*

another pretentious english group
thinking the audience is a mirror

*

on the streets again
doing my old confidence trick, trock

April 5th

      it's enough to make you
      turn in your grave

              *

a message from the stars in cancer through radio waves. oscar wilde/fingal's cave. tulips took over the dutch economy. every picture tells a story. i think, therefore thought is. descartes's/leonardo's whirlpools. re-create the past. we are the product of peoples' battles inside our heads. it has been the *presence* or *personality* of artists, not their work. that's why the academies don't like 'anecdotal'

April 8th

PICTURES, e.g. ed and me in cambridge: neil rennie, hugo and me at lunch. packet of 10 embassy. 2 gold leaf packets. '29' on building opposite. chenille lions on wall. hugo's discoloured tooth (right-hand side). flakes of (the bill was £1.97) rice (yellow) on the cloth. man in black suit (maroon (red) pocket handkerchief) talking about 'selling short', 'injecting 42 millions'. enter frank zappa, telling the truth.

April 15th

the lights of trucks at night through the jungle. val on t.v. (have GUEST STARS in the book). life as dodgems. no, dr. leary, it is NOT a film they're making. you see it is the struggle between life and mind . . . so why should mind worry about life? . . . do you see death as the world going on without you, or you releasing your threads (wires?) into the world?

April 18th

remember getting the white paper on the hola camp deaths

where is self when i am thinking of it?

April 20th

household cavalry doing drill in the sunshine to 'rain-drops keep falling on my head'

April 25th

FOR TOM CLARK

all my life i've lived before
prose is that
poetry is where at least three times

Well, that takes care of the notebook. It's eleven thirty. A plane is passing overhead. I have three cigarettes left and can get no more until four thirty. This morning I woke at six, put on jeans, denim jacket and plimsolls and started to run. The sun was bright, but it was freezing outside. In places there is still thick snow. I ran down the road, between the pine trees, to the main gate. On the way back I saw a track beside one of the lakes and ran along that. Every twenty yards or so I had to stop running and walk carefully across a patch of frozen snow. I pissed into a snow bank and wondered why I couldn't cut a pattern until I realised it was so cold that the piss was almost frozen before it hit the snow. Around the other side of the lake I took another track which led behind a house into a thick grove of pines. The trees had been planted in rows and the path led straight down the middle SHIT, I'm going up to the house to xerox this . . . and start making a carbon to send to Val so she knows what's happening.

Dear Ed: Now it's thursday lunchtime. Yesterday I did nothing but walk around this room, walk around the lakes, lie on my bed. It's the adjustment from things outer to things inner. I read two books: Ed Sanders's *Shards of God* and a book called *Policewoman* by Dorothy Uhnak.

Well, when I got down to that thick grove of pines and started to enter the trees a white owl flew straight down the centre of the path and passed exactly overhead. At the moment I was looking up, I stepped onto some level-seeming snow and sank down to my knees in it. It was the first owl I'd seen outside of a zoo. In fact I think the only other one I've ever seen was called an eagle owl and is in the zoo at Colchester in a cage, the floor of which is littered with small dead birds. I was sure I was hallucinating, so, still in the snowdrift up to my knees, I kept staring and yes, it had an owl's face. That set me up for breakfast. Something is happening to my eyes. Looking through my glasses through windows in which trees are reflected I see ghosts everywhere. As though all the people who have been here have filled the space with trace. I smoked my last joint before breakfast and sat completely paranoid. There's a Korean novelist here named Kim whose eyes are good to look through. He was saying how he'd learned English from old movies. Like Shirley Temple's 'You have to ess   em   eye   el   ee / to be aitch   ay   double pee   why.' Then the first time he left Korea and landed in America he saw a newspaper with enormous headlines saying SHIRLEY TEMPLE DIVORCED and thought 'Ohhhhh . . . these people BLIND!' The only trouble with the movies was that kissing scenes were not allowed. So every film that ended in a clinch was cut back to the previous scene. Then someone else started talking about an SDS girl who'd said 'Communism is good / capitalism is bad'...and a novelist from the South said 'What *tahm* of the *deh* was it? Oh ... *mah*nin. I thought if it was the ahfta*noon* she maht'v bin *hah* on some o that marijoo*ah*na.' So I went to my cabin, lit the stove, and wrote picture postcards of the Saratoga Racetrack to the kids. Later I went over to the house and called David and Nicole, who were good to hear. When I got back to the cabin the air inside was burning and there was a sweet smell of woodsmoke in the room.

Yesterday morning I was woken by the sound of running water . . . a leaking gutter above my window. I'd slept through the ring of the alarm clock . . . so no time for a run. At breakfast there was a letter from my father. Put it in.

8 Avondale Road, Welling, Kent. 17th April 1971.

Dear Tommy, Wherever you are when you read this we hope all goes well. We were very pleased to get your letter, and it was kind to send the book, so carefully packed (I almost threw away the letter written on the cardboard). We read it with interest (including the laudatory words on the back of the jacket) and hope it will add to your reputation. I shall try to get the Penguin book in May. There seems to have been a poetry explosion, and the resulting poeticized particles are too small for me to handle mentally with any satisfaction. Sometimes I seem to hover on the edge of a meaning to these minutiae of sensibility, but finally it eludes me. Perhaps it is a private world that I am not supposed to enter? A pity, because beauty does not lose by being shared. I hope you will not think of us as James Joyce thought of his aunt. He sent her a copy of *Ulysses*, and waited for her comments. Apparently nothing was forthcoming. So he wrote to her, and I quote: 'There is a difference between a present of a pound of chops and a present of a book like *Ulysses*. You can acknowledge receipt of the present of a pound of chops by simply nodding gracefully, supposing, that is, that you have your mouth full of as much of the chops as it will conveniently hold, but you cannot do so with a large book on account of the difficulty of fitting it into the mouth.'

We have not heard from Bridie recently, but I telephoned the hospital yesterday evening and they said she was quite comfortable.

We hope Valerie (note: he never spells her name correctly . . . that's irritated me for years . . . OK, Dad, it's VALARIE) and the children will enjoy the little change at Brighton. Valerie, I expect, will be back in Colchester in time to cope with the census form.

I had a nasty attack of the gout last week, my foot felt like a hot sponge filled with needles, but it has eased off now to a lukewarm tingling. Thank the Lord for that. I have a theory that walking is good for it, especially in the sweet spring air with the trees just breaking into leaf. I am in no hurry to exchange my lease of life for a freehold in eternity. There is plenty more of Plato to read, and then I would like to have another go at Plotinus (in a marvelous translation by Stephen McKenna, an Irishman). Your mother is at present absorbed in *Treasure Island*. She is truly omnivorous. I believe that if I gave her the London Directory she would read it (and then complain that there wasn't much plot in it).

We had a letter at Easter from Margaret, the Poor Clare (note: my cousin the nun). She seems very happy, and was called in from her wood chopping to take a telephone call from her father and mother in Australia.

There is a nice show of daffodils and hyacinths in the garden, with tulips and bluebells coming on. Your mother loves to look after the flowers, and I begin to think they love to see her.

I shall type the address in caps as I don't know if YADDO is the name of a person or a place or the initials of an organisation.

We do hope you will be able to find time to see us on your return. We scarcely recognised you in the photograph on the back of the book. I must have been thinking about your poems when I went to bed last night because I dreamed that you had exploded Bridges's 'London Snow' and I was trying to reconstruct it from the particles. Not a dream really, only the mind toying with a theme for a moment and then dropping it.

I enclose a bit of Old England – mind it doesn't disintegrate on exposure to the American air (note: enclosed was a newspaper clipping of a photograph of an old man in a top hat and knotted scarf leaning on a stick. The caption read: 'Robert Morvinson, carrier and shoemaker of Stallingborough, Lincolnshire, photographed in 1857 aged 82. This is one of 159 photographs in "A Country Camera, 1844–1914" by Gordon Winter (David and Charles, £2.25).

Morvinson was born in 1775 when Bonnie Prince Charlie was still alive.') Living with such a collection of characters must have been a perpetual feast. Carlyle used to order a box of long clay pipes from Paisley and smoke a new one every day, putting the old one on the doorstep before he went to bed to be taken by who would.

May God bless and direct you. With all good wishes . . .

I've just realised why I added that. About a year ago, when Stuart was asking me what I'd done about part two of *A Serial Biography*, I had the idea of just typing copies of every piece of mail that arrived for me for three months and sending them to him – just the incoming mail, no replies. But then for the first week all I got were bills and invitations to subscribe to *Life* and *Time* so I got bored. But the idea's been lying around there ever since. Well, dust it off, turn it around, take a photograph of its reflection, buy it a set of retreads and off it goes again. Or maybe it was my lunch today: two pieces of fried chicken, some lettuce and slices of carrot, a tub of cottage cheese and some coffee – all packed in a little black tin lunch box. I feel I'm still waiting for my soul to catch up with me. It certainly wasn't there on that Jumbo Jet watching the movie (Peter Sellers and Goldie Hawn in *There's a Girl in My Soup*). They should still run the *Queen Elizabeth*, empty but for souls. And fidgeting around on my desk I find a sheet of paper which proves me wrong about yesterday:

> beer and mind and soul and thought and transmigration of souls. woken this morning by the sound of water running . . . a leaky gutter . . . didn't hear the alarm clock so no run no nothing all day

(in the lunch pail was ham and mayonnaise, peanut butter and jelly, a banana, cottage cheese and some strips of carrot). i lit the stove . . . read 'policewoman' by dorothy uhnak. letter from my parents walked around through the woods going ankle deep in mud and came out behind my cabin . . . red squirrel going up tree (as i write red squirrel i look out of the window and a grey squirrel runs up a tree) back in the house i lay on the bed and read 'shards of god' . . . today i feel incredibly depressed goddamn it my watch is rusting there's a green stripe on the back of my hand. my plimsolls are drying on the stove what the fuck am i going to write about i better straighten my table and get down to some damn work tomorrow. i can take people in ones and twos but en masse and at dinner everyone's full of shit. take lunch pail back to house and have a shit myself

Fighting off 'characters' is taking time. The words form themselves into speeches and project faces to say them. It's like some enormous political convention inside my head. And they never rest. Last night I dreamed a book, black, with a title on the cover; and opened it and began to read. Treacherous bastards I'm going to cork you in until you understand you are PLOT not CHARACTER.

I remember the first time I saw Val. It was at noon, in the canteen of the Wellcome Foundation building, 183/193 Euston Road, London NW1. I was sitting eating lunch with Steve Fletcher. She came through the doorway, and stood at the end of the queue with a girl named Pam. She was wearing a blue (light blue) sweater and a pale grey gabardine skirt. Her hair was cut just to the level of her chin. I decided to spend the rest of my life with her. My watch IS rusty. I just took it off and looked at the back and right underneath where it says STAINLESS STEEL BACK SWISS MADE 10047 is a thin line of rust. Bastards. I bet their cuckoo clocks only go 'cuck' now. So I'm going to wash my hair and take the car in to Saratoga Springs to the post office.

Dear Ed: This is a cassette of winter 1947 (visual) with a soundtrack mostly from 1971. I wake in the morning shivering; the linoleum freezes the soles of my feet. The window is covered in ice. I have to breathe on it several times, each intake of breath chilling the back of my throat. He agrees with the Indian novelist that J. D. Salinger is one of the more interesting American writers. Ice cubes click. A refrigerator door shuts. Water sluices from a tap. He agrees to go and have a beer and a pizza. Doors slam and a car starts up. I begin to cough. There is a thick rime of ice on the sleeve of my pyjamas. It is still dark outside, the streetlamps went off at midnight. The one light bulb makes my room an orange cube of ice. Snow is thick on the ground and there is no sound. My mother comes into the room and tells me to get back into bed. She has black hair and wears an apron with a pattern of bright flowers. She brings two hot-water bottles. I get back into the cold bed, pushing one of the bottles down with my feet. Warming my hands on the other I smell the comforting scent of warm rubber. My father comes in and bends over to kiss me. He hasn't yet shaved, and smells of tobacco. He goes downstairs and begins to rake out the fire. As they wait for the pizza music blasts from the room next door where there is dancing. Another time shift: the records are all from the '50s – 'At the Hop', 'Handy Man', 'Lightning Striking Again', Freddy Cannon's 'Way Down Yonder in New Orleans'. I hear my parents talking quietly downstairs. It grows light outside. My mother comes into my room again with some newspapers and sticks and begins to lay the fire. I realise that I am ill. That's the only time a fire is lit in a bedroom. Listening to the roar of the flames I drift off to sleep. I dream he is talking about their energy terrifying her. And that the room he is in has a row of wooden tables and is crowded with students drinking beer. I dream he eats a pizza which is overcooked – the bread as hard as a biscuit. And that the Korean novelist is telling them of a pilgrimage he made as a child. Travelling for many days up into the mountains, with no money, standing each night in the snow at any gate until given a place to sleep and a little food. Until he arrived late one night at the temple and was taken in and fed. And realised that the young boy with shaven head who served him was a beautiful girl . . . and understood that he was in a nunnery . . . the head nun telling him that now he was rested he must really move on to the monastery . . . that they could not have a man sleep under their roof. Sending to guide his way the youngest novice carrying a lantern on a stick. The orange light swaying and reflecting from her bald head as they crossed the snow. I dream that as he listens to the story he thinks of a letter from his son which arrived that morning:

Dear Dad: I am writing this letter because I could not get all the news on a postcard. I am having a great time and yesterday I paid 3/- for a drive in a *real* go-kart, at the bend I put the brake on so hard the back end swung out and hit the wall.

The weather is lovely and sunny and today we are going to the waxworks (chamber of horrors) and Lisa might take a photograph. Aram has got over his 'flu by the way.

I hope it is OK in America for you. If you see a Hells Angel, take a photo for me.

I have been out with Gaynor and the family to a café and the waitress was hopeless, forgot everything. Saw a super-funny cowboy film, began like this. Out in the west are many cowboys. Some are good, some are bad. Some are bad with a bit of good in them, some are good with a bit of bad in them. This story is about some pretty good bad cowboys. See postcard.

Which has not yet arrived. I wake up. There is a roaring in the room. My mother is talking quietly to the plumber who is mending a burst pipe. It is the sound of his blowlamp I hear as he pumps up the pressure. He says something to me, but already my attention is slipping. I am thinking of the snow outside and wondering how the red fire alarm ('Penalty for False Alarm £5') opposite the corner of our street looks against it. I sleep again. And dream that he sleeps in a wicker chair in a small house near Torremolinos and wakes with 142 mosquito bites on his left arm and the left side of his face. He has dreamed of reading a sheet of typewritten paper which says:

I dreamed I was in the street (at the end): money was stolen in a tin box. I put it through the window of a house (small hole) at the same time I was the policeman who stole the money (a wad of notes) and relocked the box. I dropped the key down a drain outside King's Cross Station. Waited outside the newsagents – above which was the police headquarters – with a crowd of people, getting bored. London became France. I had had an injection. An old French lady took me in to make me a gentleman. I had to find the lavatory in the building to change my clothes. And I had to ask in French: the doorman didn't speak English. I went out to buy a copy of (   ), but there were none in the shop.

I noticed a play by (   ), a black author. Then on the street again it was New York the South and the whites were trapped in a room from which they were escaping one at a time through a window (they thought secretly), but we blacks outside were just waiting for the police chief. Whites came. We ran. I couldn't use my white car, but had to get to my wife in hospital (my small black daughter was with me). I clubbed the driver. Another man held back the passengers. I drove the coach to the outskirts of the city. A red light on the front kept flashing and by pressing two buttons I could stop it momentarily. There were only six or seven passengers in the back. I was worried that the radio would transmit. Cut. I was walking back to the coach. When I opened the door it was filled with people and I knew the driver had gone for the police. We mingled with the crowd and, crossing the first street, I saw the police station and the driver talking to the police outside (all wearing different-coloured long raincoats). It seemed easy to find one black man and a small girl with pigtails. I went into the subway but there was only one line, alongside the east edge of the city, and no transfers. The chart was a map of the city covered with trees.

I wake again and it is night. My father is home from work and sits on a chair beside my bed. A wooden chair, with a curved back and a seat of plywood patterned with small holes. He switches on the light and begins to read to me from *What the Moon Saw*.

The dream was over, and although he understood that with the half of his mind that had paused to wonder why he had begun the sentence, he knew that the letters had to go on and on to the end . . . like the glass circling and circling the ouija board . . . an order of ritual that would cease only when the green gulls, finishing their last flight, circled for the final time and landed, breaking their legs on the sheet of thick plate glass stretched two feet above the ground. Oh, the surprise on their faces when gas jets lit beneath the glass and they sizzled their way into eternity. That's all it is.

I found a dead mouse in the woodpile today, curled among some leaves. I thought at first it was asleep, hibernating, but when I lifted it it was stiff. I've moved it onto the window ledge beside the catch, while I think what to do with it. The more formless I try to be, the more objects push themselves into a shape. I went up to the house a few minutes back to make some phone calls . . . I talked to Harvey . . . then got no reply from your number . . . no reply from Tom Clark's. So I went into the library to check on that 'London Snow' poem. I found a collected Bridges on the shelf, and as I was reaching for it something distracted me. When I opened the book in my hand I read Chief Joseph:

> Hear me, my warriors; my heart is sick and sad.
> Our chiefs are killed,
> The old men are all dead.
> It is cold, and we have no blankets;
> The little children are freezing to death.
> Hear me, my warriors; my heart is sick and sad.
> From where the sun now stands I will fight no
>   more forever.

We are exactly on the borderline of the seasons. This morning there was snow: now the sun is out and warm. Through the window I see the blue smoke from my chimney blowing down through the trees towards the highway. I can't hit any rhythm yet . . . I feel like an android . . . or a car that has been converted from petrol to natural gas. Last night I clearly remember dreaming that I found a bag of cocaine in the hem of my blanket, but someone knocked it from my hand. It fell onto a piece of white carpet, and I was down on my hands and knees picking all over the white fluff sniffing at my fingertips. Every stupid remark I've heard surfaces and demands to be reheard. The schoolteacher in London who was asking little kids to write poems (I mean she was 'modern' . . . that's one good thing about sociology . . . it's given the enemy a bright red uniform . . . their own blood may not show when they're hit, but we're fighting in the forest now, so can see them coming and there's time to get away) and told me, 'You know, some of them turned in these RHYMING POEMS. I said, "Children, you *will* write FREE VERSE!"' Or the women's lib girl at the university telling Val, 'You *can't* be happy doing that . . . you *must* go out and see some *fo*reign *films!*' Or Dudley Young saying he believed the most important things in life were 'manners, decorum and style', as if he knew what any one of the three words meant. The room is filled with a golden light: the tall trees clatter their branches in the wind. Beside me the stove crackles, and occasionally pops. The mouse stares at me: I think I'll leave it there.

Dear Ed: Put in the paper and burn off. So the talk after dinner last night got down to universities and grades and the differences between the French, English and American systems of grading. You dig, like that's the formal penance for being inside your head all day. And people were conscientious. Suddenly Korean voice speak out: 'American grades I don like. Students come, they say "Mr. Kim, where I stand?" I say "You standin in my room, man." I say to students "'A' is used too much . . . we give other letters a chance." So I put an "F" and student say "Mr. Kim, I have to show this to my parent." I tell him "'F' mean FINE when I put it . . . and 'A' mean Awfully Anaemic." Girl come to me she say "I pregnant" . . . I tell her "Don WORRY . . . I give you all A's." Boy tell me his father die . . . I say "You just bring me one sheet of writing, you have A." As he turn to go I see hole in his shoe. "Forget about sheet of writing" I tell him. American teachers come out of room waving hands saying "Not enough time . . . I need more time to tell them everything." I go into class . . . after twenty minutes, nothing more to say. They read essays so carefully . . . making little marks and comments. I read through all of it fast and if I don like, I put B.S., bullshit, on the bottom.'

Pouring with rain. I have to get some more logs for the stove (it's called, by the way, VOLCANO 222). No postcard from Lloyd this morning. 'This story is about some good bad cowboys. See postcard' is almost as irritating as a telegram saying IGNORE FIRST TELEGRAM. So let's get into something else. I walked back from the house looking down at the pine cones. How ridiculous to see everything from where your head is. Fibre-optics should make it possible to have spectacles like antennae . . . now moving along one inch from the ground looking right and left at your own feet . . . now looking ahead with one and behind with the other . . . now looking down at your own head. Or how about stretching them out in front of you, then turning the tips and looking at yourself walking forwards. That would *really* make the background move, and rinse out your brain. Form is content stretched to whatever shape fits best against the backcloth given by time—so *that* is the set where the *real* action is. If time is like a back projection of change, then what is the screen on which it's focus'd? Let's jam the projector and let the beam burn a bright hole through one still frame of time. I wonder when the first meeting was arranged. When did encounters cease to be random? What fool first said 'I'll meet you by that rock when the sun next rises' . . . no . . . it would be something like 'when you see again after the blackness' . . . some shit like that? If I follow *this* track I'll end up working out a code of grunts. To use an old form for a new content is like making the work a mnemonic for children. Each small piece of, for instance, the poem, is fastened down with little boring arrows pointing at it from all directions. But H.O.M.E.S. is not the Great Lakes. He said boringly. Let's break out of that.

I got up to measure this room, to start describing it. Seven easy paces from door to stove: eight the other way, from wall to wall. But then I caught myself whistling the first few bars of Dizzy Gillespie's 'Night in Tunisia' over and over again. Somewhere that tape had been switched in. I remember the first time I really heard jazz was during my second year in grammar school. That would be '51 or '52. How strange . . . I'm trying to think of the names of the two boys who had the records . . . I can seem them clearly – even to the burn on the smaller one's left arm where a Very flare he'd found during the war and lit with a match had exploded. But all I can remember is CHUCK and HANK which they chalked on the upturned peaks of their school caps. The school had a semi-compulsory music society, very straight. I can smell the polish and feel myself wriggling in my chair as another chunk of cultural fudge was pushed my way. Then Chuck came in with a record . . . I can see the red and white label now. And said it was a new work by a young French composer named Giles Spie called 'Le Champ', The Field. He explained how, if everyone listened carefully, mice could be heard moving around in sheaves of corn. Everyone bent dutifully forward and then this beautiful noise burst out of the speaker. The unexpected expression of a truth I'd always known. Bullshit! What a pretentious sentence. Like 'the wind of time blows ripples across her face'. I'll have to be more careful. They're trying sneak attacks today. And of course it was through going to jazz clubs later that I smoked my first dope. That would be in '55 or '56. Yes, all you worried parents were right. A ten-shilling packet of grass I got from Dave Robinson who got it from a spade in the Americana Club (underneath the Mapleton Restaurant, Leicester Square) named Shiny, or Snowy . . . one of those names. No . . . not

Snowy: I remember he was one of the gang from the Elephant. Once I saw him run a sharpened nail file down someone's cheek outside the Lyceum. Dave Robinson looked like a cross between Humphrey Lyttelton and Andrzej Pluskowski. He married a girl named Jeanette who'd inherited some thousands of pounds, and went into the property business. It was Dave who first took me to the Star (known as the Scar) Club and I was so gauche I ate the sandwich that was left permanently on the table so they could serve drinks after hours 'with food'. So by 1957 I was working in London all day, getting the train home, changing my suit, getting the train back to London, spending until 2:00 a.m. in the clubs, catching the milk train (that went first to Gravesend, at the mouth of the Thames, and only stopped at my station at 4:00 a.m., on the way back to town) home, sleeping until seven – then the whole round again. Eating methedrine tablets by the handful, and weighing 126 lbs. I remember giving Vic Schonfield 200 methedrine in a Zubes cough sweet tin outside Bush House so his friends could compare them with Dexedrine. No, John Lennon, you were not alone. That would be about the middle of 1960, no, early '61. I met Vic through Pete Brown, and Pete through Mike Horovitz, and Mike through Anselm Hollo. And I met Anselm in January '61, because Val was in hospital having Lisa at the time. And how all that started was again through jazz. Sometime late in 1957 I went into Zwemmers in Charing Cross Road and bought a copy of *Evergreen Review* 2 because it had an article on jazz in San Francisco. I walked down Charing Cross Road, crossed the Strand, bought a ticket to Welling at the station and walked to the end of Platform 2 out into the weak sunshine. And into Ginsberg and Spicer.

It's the next day. I find this in my typewriter and look up and outside my window a small bird is walking down a vertical tree trunk. My ignorance worries me. I think I don't know the name of any tree, or any bird. I sit in this room surrounded by things I can name . . . thermos, photograph, jacket, pen, stove, lamp, chair . . . and through the ten windows as I swivel round I see things I can only group together as trees and birds. But the squirrels save me.

The pine needles on the snow have the same pattern as hairs that stick to the bowl after shaving. I walk round through the woods with Kim, who's leaving tomorrow. 'Everybody want to be last thief' he says. 'Take land from Indian, but then hold on tight.' A car pulls up with four men in it. 'This road go all the way round?' the driver asks. Then 'You Japanese? Oh . . . I was in Korea. Where you from?' 'D.M.Z.' Kim answers. We walk round through the rose garden and across the lawn. Where the snow has cleared the grass is pressed flat – it's like walking over slightly damp shredded wheat. He gives me half a jar of Maxwell House coffee and some slices of chicken.

Dear Ed: Adrift and alone for two days now inside my head with no shore on which to land. Speed pushes mind around in time until the scabs break off and the raw meat of thought flinches. I saw Ralphy in that small hot room on 8th Street with Roz and Pauline sitting me down on the bed, giving me a tumblerful of whisky in my right hand, a joint in my left hand, rushing over to the stereo and coming back with the headphones, putting them on me: then all of us laughing for minutes as he realised what he'd done, and I sat there, hands, mouth, nose and head full. I saw the Pacific again for the first time as I ran down the beach drunk, at one in the morning, away from the lights and towards the sound of the waves – ran straight into the sea so that for days I could taste salt and my jeans shrank and stiffened and had to be thrown away.

> as light has speed we are always
> visually in the past   as you read
> lettuce   this page may be a lettuce

I wandered around the grounds and the buildings, writing THE END with a stick in snow banks. Then I went into the house, and in a nest of drawers found a stereoscope and hundreds of pictures. I spent two hours staring into those worlds, picking the sepia photos at random. Going from '10802 – Snowcrowned Popocatépetl and Iztaccíhuatl Guarding Cathedral, Puebla, Mexico' (Keystone View Company, Manufacturers and Publishers, Medaville, Pa., St. Louis, Mo. Copyright 1900 by B. T. Singley), through '13319 – The Flower of Venezuela's Regular Army' and '11064 – Killing the Fatted Calf, Palestine' to 'Cuban Lovers – Courting through the Barred Windows' (Underwood & Underwood, Publishers. New York, London, Toronto – Canada, Ottawa – Kansas. Works and Studios – Arlington, N.J., Littleton, N.H., Washington, D.C. Trade Mark SUNSCULPTURE). Some of the pictures had texts on the back:

In legendary tales of Puebla's (Poo-a-blah) birth, we read how this delightful spot was first made known to its founder in a wonderful dream which pictured the real, not in fancy, but as God truly made it, a beautiful plain bordered everywhere by the enrapturing splendor of mountain majesty.

With a population of 90,000, Puebla is classed among the principal cities of the republic in thrift and size. So profusely is it studded by beautiful old churches with massive walls and towering domes of various colours, that by many it is well called 'The City of Churches', but is more commonly known as 'The City of Angels'.

Save the capital, no other city of the Republic has seen more of the vicissitudes of war, and between 1821–67, it was captured and occupied six different times – by Iturbide in 1821, by Scott in 1847, and was the scene of Zaragoza's victory, May 5th, 1862, when with 2,000 men he repulsed 6,000 French soldiers, who reentered the following year only to be driven out and captured by General Díaz, April 2, 1867.

From here can be seen three of the world's greatest extinct volcanoes, Popocatépetl, Iztaccíhuatl, and the peak of Orizaba.

or

The father in the story of the Prodigal Son was so glad at the return of his lost boy, that he prepared a feast for him. He ordered him to be clothed in a new garment, to be adorned with a ring on his hand. For the feast he ordered the best which the house could offer, to be prepared, the fatted calf. The parable intends, of course, to show the feelings of the Heavenly Father for the returning sinner. This picture may give us a better understanding as to what the procedure was in slaughtering the animal. The animal is first caught and bound, and then killed.

No. It's still a day for drifting – but in a submarine through the many-coloured swirling oils. If it's done with truth and love and no wish to profit, in any sense, then it will take shape. The final thing I find in any art that moves me is the clear message: 'there is no competition because I am myself, and through that the whole.'

This morning I come back to this page and that last part is really heavy – but I feel low, so let's keep on with it. I've just eaten an orange and put the peel to dry on top of the stove so I can smell it. I put Clara Bow in the window – that way I can read both sides. This morning I had a letter from Marco Antonio, part of which says:

> I've sent you my long book, *Collected Poems* to the University. Here it has been received with much verbal enthusiasm . . . but little written criticism. I wonder if it was worth the trouble, and the twenty years I spent writing it.

and he knows as he writes that the whole point is that there *are* no rewards. The pain, the depression, the loneliness are the flesh of the oyster: that's what poets taste like. And the relief is when a fleck of sand enters and the layers of pearl start building up, taking your attention away from your self. There is no feedback from where we are . . . nothing ahead that can throw back an echo. We sit in silence waiting for the faintest sounds which are the fragments of the name of god. And when they rise we follow them wherever they go. As last night I followed them into the library, pulled down Maritain's *Creative Intuition in Art and Poetry* (and when else would I even *look* at a book like that?), opened it at random, and started reading a poem of Hart Crane's:

> Yes, I being
> the terrible puppet of my dreams, shall
> lavish this on you –

I live in a country whose poets are afraid of the dark and the wind because they carry burning books outside which are soon blown out. They have forgotten how to carry a coal, which gives more light as the wind blows. Even the best of them withdraw from what they know they should do. The crack is there in front of them, but they're not sure if they can survive on the other side. They wait for a messenger to arrive and face them, reading out a list of houses, flats, bus schedules, and the prices of canned foods. And every day the gap widens – and there are no poles left with which to vault across, and no planks over which to crawl, because the trees have long ago been cut down and made into paper for the books they thought would light their way.

You see this is not spontaneous . . . it is talking when there is talk there. Kerouac was the last to try and get all the way round before the bell rang for time. I sleep much more heavily here: the characters and words will somehow act their parts.

Dear Ed: Art is making new games: that's the message for today. Let me tell you about my regular life here. I've trained myself (now *that's* a ridiculous phrase if you look at it) during the past week to wake at five to seven. At seven o'clock I start running past the garage, down through the woods and around the lakes. I am back at the house around seven fifteen. I wash, make my bed and walk to the garage building for breakfast. Each day I have a glass of orange juice, cornflakes with cold milk, two scrambled eggs, and two cups of coffee. Then I leave any mail I've written in the basket by the door and collect any that's arrived. I walk back to the house, read the mail in my bedroom, go down to the kitchen to collect my lunch pail and thermos, then walk to my cabin. There I clean the ashes out of the stove, light the fire with the paper yesterday's food was wrapped in (plus any scraps from my wastepaper basket) and some kindling from a cardboard carton. I then read my mail again, by which time the kindling has caught, and I can put a couple of logs into the stove from the rack in the corner of the room. I usually look out of the window for a while, at the trees and the birds and the squirrels. I crumble up whatever cake or cookie is in the lunch pail and throw it out of the door. Then I listen to the traffic for a while. I can just see the highway through the trees. After that I sweep the floor and write letters. At four o'clock I take my lunch things back to the kitchen and read in my bedroom until five thirty, when I go down to the kitchen, make a drink, and take it into the library. Dinner is at six thirty. Back to the house at eight. Make some phone calls. Drink some more. Go to bed. At least that's the theory. Well, we're all going to die, that's for sure. Like the mouse that hasn't moved.

Names and shapes are getting used up fast, that's why the gap is growing. And anyone left over on that other side will be inside a faulty machine. As the child grows and the parents die, so does the machine we are in produce its successor. It is not self-repairing: it wants to die, and any attempt at patching it up turns its anger against the repairers. When, by a series of coincidences, I walk into the lounge at the airport in Toronto and sitting in front of me is Jean Blondel you can't kid me that the machine hasn't momentarily run out of shapes and had to flash him in there. Like going in yesterday evening to post a letter to you and first passing a truck with DORN in large letters on the side, then turning a corner and stopping beside an oil drum with DIVERSEY stencilled on it. Like Bradley and Barnett being two players in a basketball game I watched on t.v. And Barnet being the place where Peter Bradley (who once lent me £50 which I still owe him) lived when I first met him . . . and where Val and I lived for three years six years after . . . and in the same street, Manor Road. He was a biochemist; but had a few sidelines, like making a liquid methedrine and barbiturate mixture, making his own liquor from pure alcohol and orange peel, and growing his own grass. The grass was the only stuff I've ever hallucinated on. He didn't know how to cure or dry it, so he chopped it into fine pieces (like mint before it goes into a sauce) and smoked it like that. You had to smoke about a pack of twenty, and in a closed room, but then it hit you like a train. I liked him. He was quiet, and bright, and pleasant. But his parties were a drag – he was into candles, Dylan Thomas records, traditional jazz, and Greek folk music. It was at one of his parties that I met Jeff Nuttall. (By the way, it has to be nomadic over the gap . . . so the luggage will be much lighter.)

He stops to watch the smoke rising from his cigarette and to scrape his chair back. Looking to his left he reads on a yellow pad with thin blue lines 'LEWIS: 2031 B. Oak St., San. Fran. 94117'. The fire cracks once. Outside the window, to his right, leaves blow and four dark birds peck amongst them. As he looks and thinks of that sentence, a brilliant red bird lands on a thin pine tree. The first brightly coloured bird he has ever seen free. Cardinal comes into his head, and on the yellow pad he writes 'cardinal?' He taps the tip of his pen on the desk, then starts a little drum solo. Putting his cigarette in the glass ashtray to the right of the typewriter he drinks his coffee.

In 1955 Ray Collingwood and I decided to go to sea. So we got a trolleybus (696) down to Woolwich and went into the docks. We wandered around for an hour or so, looking at the cranes and wondering why there were two men's lavatories, one marked ORIENTALS. Then we boarded a couple of ships, talked to a few people – but no one would take us on. There was conscription then, and many boys went into the merchant navy to avoid the army . . . although you had to stay in until you were (I think) twenty-six to avoid military service completely. So there was a law that you couldn't join if you were over seventeen. We ate our lunch in the dockers' canteen, talked for a while, then decided that if we had to do our two years in whatever branch of the army we were pushed into, we might as well volunteer for three years, get more money, and pick where we wanted to go. Outside the docks we caught a bus to Blackheath (can't remember the number) and went to the recruiting office. It was just around the corner from my old school; next to the stop where, a few years before, Brian

Simmons, Kevin Considine and I used to spend our dinner money on those round chocolate truffle cakes with little chocolate needles all over them. I forget completely what happened to Ray, but the sergeant explained to me all about travel and then asked me what I wanted to join. The Parachute Regiment, I told him. He told me I didn't weigh enough. When I left the office I had an appointment for a medical, and a reservation in the rifle regiment. But I never took it up: at the medical the doctor told me I had a hole in my heart, so I spent the next few months on the dole waiting to go into hospital.

I was friendly with Brian Simmons because he liked science fiction. We had our trousers narrowed to 14" bottoms and bought slim-jim ties in Lewisham – black, about an inch and a half wide, with thin diagonal lurid violet stripes. After a week, we were called up one morning in assembly and our clothes were pointed out as not the way the school uniform should be worn. But we didn't change, and no more was said. There were two boys with red hair in the class: a fat one named Brendan Murphy who impressed me one day by bringing his father's Beretta automatic to school in a handkerchief, and letting me click it a few times . . . and a boy named Raven who had a seemingly inexhaustible supply of money. I started going around with him in 1954. I am sure his parents must have had a shop, and he stole from the till – because he wasn't rich (not with those bright blue double-breasted suits with 24" trouser bottoms). We would skip school at the eleven o'clock break and take the train from Blackheath to Charing Cross. Then in Lyon's Strand Corner House we'd eat an enormous lunch surrounded by middle-class middle-aged ladies, while a string quartet played behind some palms. Those were the times I began to drink. We thought cocktails were sophisticated, so we'd order maybe three different ones, throughout the meal. Manhattans . . . Sidecars . . . the very names were so sharp. Then we'd go to the pictures and catch a train back that would get us home around the usual time. I would do anything to avoid school that last year, 1954. It drove me mad to sit in those classrooms. I was going out with a girl named Pat who lived in the next street to me, and who I'd first kissed during a game of Postman's Knock at a party in the house next door when I was twelve. At eight o'clock I had to leave my house to catch the bus (89) to Blackheath. She went to school at Bexleyheath, about ten minutes away by trolleybus (696 again), so I'd hang around until eight thirty, walk her to the bus stop, ride in to Bexleyheath, and walk her down to school. Then I'd go over to the golf course and sit for a while . . . or walk along the Broadway looking at the shops. At noon I'd go back down to the school to meet her, and we'd go to the golf course and neck. In the afternoon I'd take the bus back into Welling and read in the Reference Library until four thirty. Then I'd meet her at the bus stop and go home.

The point must lie where 'like' slides into 'is'. I found the quote for this book late last night, in Trelawny's *Recollections of the Last Days of Shelley and Byron*:

> Infidel, jacobin, leveller: nothing can stop this spread of blasphemy but the stake and the faggot; the world is retrograding into accursed heathenism and universal anarchy!

Yes, the wheel turns full circle: but the flaw in the rim touches the ground each time in a different place. And for ten years all I have done has been an adolescent's game, like the bright feathers some male birds grow during the mating season. I look at the poems and they make up a museum of fragments of truth. And they smell of vanity, like a hunter's trophies on the wall ('I shot that poem in '64, in France.'). I have never reached the true centre, where art is pure politics.

It is two in the morning, one day in 1964. I am sitting in the fluorescent glare of the canteen at the top of the Faraday Building, near St. Paul's Cathedral, where the Continental and International telephone exchanges are. I am talking to Viv Nixson, who went through the Continental training for thirteen weeks with me, and to Gene Mahon, who works in International, and who I met once, years before, when he went out with a girl named Joan Finch who sat opposite me in an office in Euston Road. Years later Viv will be theatre manager of the Victoria Theatre, Stoke-on-Trent, and Gene will design the label for Apple Records. We are exhausted. We've been working since five thirty the previous evening: a duty which should have finished at eleven, but we've extended it (for the overtime) into an all-night . . . which means we leave at 8:00 a.m. During the night we have a break of two hours, from midnight until two, or from two until four. At the corner tables groups of Mauritians are playing cards. To work in Continental you have to speak reasonable French, and as the Mauritians are French-speaking, with dual British and French nationality, many of them work here. At two thirty we go down to the basement and play snooker. The light over the green table and the click of the balls are relaxing after the flashing red, green, white and orange lights of the exchange, and the glare of the canteen. At four I go back to work. Several operators are sitting at their positions around the multiple, and a couple of supervisors are talking quietly at their table in the centre of the room. I am working on Ship to Shore, in the corner. Plugging in my headset I lean on my left elbow, hold an answering cord ready in my right hand, and try to doze. A supervisor shouts 'One up!' I look at the multiple and a white light glows for a second or two, then vanishes. I hear an operator down the room say sleepily 'Continentalservicenumberplease.' At eight the previous evening, when the exchange was blazing with lights from incoming calls, a subscriber would have had to wait maybe ten minutes for an answer. Now, early in the morning, when he would have been prepared to wait a little, his phone rings for perhaps three seconds. The supervisor's keenness reminds me now of the Union of Post Office Workers official who said to me when the postmen were working to rule, and consequently the telephone system was flooded with calls, 'What . . . and lose all this overtime!' when I mentioned some vague idea of solidarity. But I liked the job. Apart from the usual civil service shit, and the 200 different varieties of tickets to fill out for calls, you were finally left pretty much to yourself. I would 'accidentally' disconnect people whose voices I didn't like, or who were rude to me. I would let girls phoning their soldier boyfriends in Germany for three minutes from a call box (just over 10/-) talk for perhaps ten minutes, instead of cutting them off. One Christmas I linked the East Berlin operator to the West Berlin operator and let them talk. And there were always interesting calls to overhear. If you ever call your girlfriend at three in the morning and the volume gradually goes down, picture in your mind ten bored operators with nothing to do but over-plug your circuit, sit back, and listen. We invented games to pass the time. A telephone number picked at random would be handed round and, in turn, at one-hour intervals, we'd call the number and ask for Joe. At six in the morning, whoever made the last call would say 'This is Joe . . . any messages?' For a month, every time I was working all night, I'd call the British Embassy in Paris on one line, and Orly Airport on the other: then pull the monitor key back and listen . . . at four in the morning. Or I'd find a number with a tape recorder connected for messages (like Westminster Abbey at night) and fill the tape with scraps of conversation, the weather forecast in French, the time signal, and pop records you could get by dialling certain numbers in Germany. Back in 1964 the phone rings on the supervisor's desk. It is 7:30 a.m. now. I am called over, and pick up the receiver. It's Val. She tells me a letter has just arrived from the landlords and we are being evicted from our flat that morning.

He is riding in a red car through what seems to be a desert. In the distance is a tall white building. Parking the car on some cinders he goes through a stone gateway, along a path bordering some brown grass, buys a ticket and enters the building. Paintings crumble on the walls. He climbs the stairs inside and comes out onto a ledge. Music from a transistor radio rises from behind a wall. Leaving, he gets into the wrong car.

Sunday is sunday everywhere. Even here, isolated, the difference must be made: breakfast is at eight thirty instead of at eight. In the *New York Times Magazine* there's a piece about the new relevance of comics . . . which to illustrate its point says something like 'Students at Yale read extracts over their radio station' – which seems to be the opposite of what the man thinks he means. I pin a few things to my wall: a poster for a reading by Tom Veitch and Clark Coolidge . . . your drawing of the SS *Panama*. The day after tomorrow David is driving over from Northampton to take me back there for a couple of days. I remember when I met him, in Anselm's flat in 1961, he was just starting his doctorate at the Sorbonne. Now, on the phone, he tells me it's finished . . . he's just completed the bibliography. So the '60s are over at last. I am back in the exchange. Our evening duties end at ten, ten thirty or eleven. If we're not busy, we're released ten minutes early. I discover that if I touch the tip of my answering cord to the edge of a socket, the light above goes out – while the caller still hears a ringing tone. At ten forty-five the multiple is a blaze of lights. I run the tip of my cord along three rows of answering sockets. Every light goes out. We are released. Across the country people listen to the ringing tone, cursing.

Dear Ed: It's so grey here: five days of rain, mist in the mornings. The air in the cabin is green, with small flecks of gold wherever the light from my lamp hits a metal window catch or some other reflecting surface. Through a thin crack in the top of the stove I see the bright flames dancing inside. Trucks pass along the highway I can barely see through the trees, but my chair vibrates. It feels like Christmas when I was five. I shut myself inside the circle of light and go back to 1953. Dates blow off a calendar: a few clouds scud by. I am running up the stairs. The carpet is worn through and the stair rods clatter in their sockets. On the landing at the top is my Uncle Arthur. I have a piece of paper in my hand, my head is burning. 'Look!' I say to him, 'look what I've written!' He takes the paper, and I remember the poem now:

> o what fun
> to be a boy
> and have a toy
>
> i teach my soldiers to fight
> and my lions to bite
>
> o what fun
> to be a boy
> and have a toy

the first thing I ever wrote. 'Copied' he says, continuing downstairs, 'you must have copied it from somewhere – you couldn't have written it.' The valves that blew out in my head then are still dead. I shine the torch around over them but they can't be repaired. I feel the wall under my hands, the roughness of the stippled distemper. I taste the powder in my mouth as I bite my nails and try to tell him 'I DID write it!' And so I lose my faith in truth. Well, everyone you punch at is the same shape. Maybe that's in some perverted way why I keep the dead mouse on my windowsill.

timber	truck	vibrates
my	s	pine

is how I'd write it now, I suppose.

One year later, 1944, at school. I go into the lavatory from the playground to piss. Three boys I've not seen before are standing just inside the door. 'Here' one of them calls to me 'have you ever seen a match burn twice?' Interested, I go over. He strikes a match, blows out the flame, and presses the hot tip to the back of my hand. I scream. They run off laughing. I lose my trust in people. Well, from the point of view of shadows there is no light.

> i lose
> my faith
> in truth
> i lose
> my trust
> in people

is how I'd write it now, I suppose.

Let me send you a copy of a novel I wrote last year (if I sent it before, this is where it belongs). It's called:

PLASTIC SPOON   a novel

t.v. is out of focus, or so the watch swings
i mean he is examining it, taking a cigarette, looking
voice says 'the picture of indian face' wind, wind
he hears it behind, swinging bleached out in the window

peddler sings 'nothin'. . . I just wanna talk t'yuh'
'come up'n sit'n the (now let i deviate

holding three kings : this is now, seven p.m.
the poem the variations the will the spring the from

*

blur   blur
what's that?   oh
sepia screw
take a spin in the focal length

bicycle days (or: a telegram)
la   la   la   LA   la   la   la

*

with a flurry of spoke he whirled on his
machine   gravel spurt
                  we are at large
in the machine, and the colours today
are green (with a dash of yellow at the
centre) rose (with a dash of blue
at the edge) and the colour exactly
between green and blue

*

dank day   a good day   for english poetray

*

as light has speed we are always
visually in the past   as you read
lettuce   this page may be a lettuce

*

attaching my klein bottle to my möbius belt i entered
königsberg (later kaliningrad) . . . soon i would be
helping count buffon with his 'needle problem'

*

some of you older children may see
the floors in my argument.   mind the edge

*

if this text is a halftone, imagine it as a line block:
enter through the 'o' in 'tone' or 'block'. now you are
beneath the page – meet me by the coca-cola sign,
or 'egress'

*

out of step (laughter) normal
for most people (titters) now, in
a crash helmet and boiler suit
(doo doo doo in tuba tones) she
applies a false moustache (apple pie)

*

what goes on in the real world

*

*

he's gone into him self! trails of ash,
fragments of paper, stop at the edge
of his sucked outline in air. he
detaches his retina: the guide dogs
run wild. in his ear he beats in morse
with the hammer on the anvil 'a roomful
of lettuce rendered into one syringe: the
man who turned yellow drinking carrot juice'

*

fool who invented the wheel because
he couldn't wait to get there quicker

*

blur blur   blur blur
what's what's that that!!   oh oh
                    crew crew

*

eight bells   each day polish my bicycle
radio waves pass through bodies
causing cancer   waves of colour t.v.
cause blood clots   medicine leaves nature
no choice but new diseases
seven bells   one bell   silent typing

*

my bicycle shape's $^co{}^1a$ i bought it
from a stylite   the shape
of its back wheel makes it uncomfortable to ride

*

blur   blur   coming up fast
it overtakes him as they blend into the window
play with marked watches the set
is switched off the images deviate life
goes on in the album   for the record
our noises are off

Dear Ed: It was good to hear you. I'm sorry if I sounded chilly on the phone. Being alone all this time, and fragmenting myself back into the past, I've grown paranoid about the Outside Present. I can cope with letters (in fact I need them very much) and phone calls I make – but the immediacy of calls coming from outside throws me into a defensive position. And I'm wary about taking anything except the work itself while I'm working. That's the dope I'm using now. I'm going on the vague notion that if I can correctly and completely describe my self, then that self will wither and blow away. Unless when you have created your self you die. Or unless we really are the hosts for some other force that sits inside us like the trainee pilot in a simulator – and similarly walks back into the world after the so-real crash.

He remembers the banana in his hand as his palm grows cold.

In February 1971 I get off the train from Colchester at Liverpool Street and walk towards the taxi rank. As I pass the news kiosk a small old man, wearing a dirty fawn raincoat and carrying a brown paper bag, stops me. 'You Jewish?' he asks. I tell him no. 'Speak German?' 'A little,' I answer. He gives me a piece of lined paper, torn from a small notebook. On it is written an address in Cazenove Road, Stoke Newington. I walk back with him to the ticket office. In a mixture of German and Yiddish he tells me he has come from Paris, where he stayed two days, and before that from Russia. At the ticket window he takes an old purse from his pocket. There are a few coins in it . . . perhaps eight or nine shillings. I buy him a ticket to Stoke Newington. Then I realise what he's saying. 'AinundZwansikjahre.' Twenty-one years in a labour camp. I go with him to the barrier, point out the train, and tell him it will leave in ten minutes. We shake hands and I walk away. I am going to the press to see Barry and sign some books.

I meet him and we go for a drink. He tells me about the old Elvis Presley English Concert rip-off. How a hall was booked, tickets printed, advertisements and posters sent out – without Presley ever having been approached. Half the tickets were sold straight, and half at inflated prices on the black market. Then it was announced that unfortunately the concert had to be cancelled. The straight money was refunded through the ticket agencies . . . and the money from the black market tickets was pure profit. We go back, smoke a joint, and I look at the stack of fifty books. I tell him I can't sign them, and go home.

I remember the pains in the back of my neck and my spine after sitting on the floor for six hours setting type. I remember setting a complete page of a story by Fielding Dawson, getting up, stumbling, and kicking the whole thing over. I remember Val taking copies of the magazine and the books round the stores in a paper carrier bag and being told 'Oh . . . we don't take things like THAT . . . we only stock REAL poetry.' Nothing to do with selling your signature.

I went for a walk up to the house after writing that to see if the sunlight would do anything. After this week of rain the light this morning hurts my eyes. Up in my room I started to look through a book called *Dancers, Buildings and People in the Streets* by Edwin Denby, and came across three paragraphs (mainly about de Kooning) which seem to accurately reflect my feelings today.

> In the presence of New York at the end of the thirties, the paranoia of surrealism looked parlor-sized or arch. But during the war Bill told me he had been walking uptown one afternoon and at the corner of 53rd and 7th he had noticed a man across the street who was

making peculiar gestures in front of his face. It was Breton and he was fighting off a butterfly. A butterfly had attacked the Parisian poet in the middle of New York. So hospitable nature is to a man of genius.

Recently a young painter walking at night down Third Avenue near 10th Street, saw him running fast. The young man wondered why de Kooning was running so fast at night. The he saw Lisbeth, de Kooning's little daughter. They were playing hide-and-seek.

"I'm not so crazy about my style," he said to me recently, "I'd just as soon paint some other way." When he was in Rome last autumn, he told me, he met at a party an American painter of his age, dignified and well dressed, with a nice wife and college son. They were making the rounds of museums and the ruins, they knew all there was to see, and enjoyed looking at it intelligently. Bill said that when he was young he expected he would later turn into a man such as that, but somehow it hadn't happened.

I never did describe this room, though I gave you the measurements. The floor is wooden, painted grey, as is the skirting board. The walls and the ceiling (high, pointed) are white. The door is in the centre of the wall to my right. It is wooden, stained, as are all the window frames. There is a window either side of the door, two windows in the wall opposite me, two in the wall to my left (between which is the stove), and four behind me. I sit at my desk, facing the centre of the room, on a wooden chair. Slightly behind me, and to my left, is a tall metal lamp. Beside it are the log rack, and cardboard boxes of kindling. Between the kindling and the stove are a white metal and plastic chair and a bucket filled with ashes. The stove stands in a wooden tray full of sand, and there is a bent brown metal reflecting screen behind it. To the right of the stove is a bookcase, empty but for an aerosol fire extinguisher. A brown wood rocking chair with a cane bottom stands in front of the shelves. In the left-hand corner of the room, facing me, is a cane armchair next to a low wooden table with curved legs on which stand a small lamp, my lunch pail, and a thermos flask (red). Against the wall, between the two windows opposite me, is another bookcase, with a few books on the top shelf and some photographs of Val and the kids. A square wooden armchair with an adjustable back and two white cushions is in the centre of the room. In the right-hand corner is a metal daybed with a light green and white paisley patterned cover and a white rough linen pillow. To the right of my desk is a small table with a glass ashtray on it, and underneath, my wastepaper basket. In the corner behind me, to my right, a small cupboard (white) with no door holds a broom and dustpan. Beams of sunlight fall across the bed and the cane armchair.

He is lying on a hospital bed. A nurse has given him an injection in his left arm and a catheter tube is being inserted into the artery inside the bend of his elbow. He is conscious, but feels nothing. The nurse wipes his forehead. In the background machines click and whir. He cannot see what is happening: in the silver shades of the overhead lamps he sees only a distorted picture. The tube penetrates further. He feels a tickling somewhere inside his left shoulder. Then nothing more. Suddenly his heart kicks. The tube has reached it and is probing inside.

It is a saturday morning in the spring of 1958. Colin Medhurst, Bob Hawkins, Mickey Annett and I walk through Leicester Square. We cross New Coventry Street and go up Wardour

Street. Opposite the Flamingo Club is an expensive shoe store. We go in and Colin buys a pair of dark brown leather italian shoes with short pointed toe caps. We cross to the doorway of the Flamingo to see who's playing that evening: then walk through Berwick Street market. At the end of the street, just before it meets Oxford Street, is Sam Arkus, the tailor. Bob is going to pick up a new suit. We go downstairs and he tries it on. It's a dark-blue wool/worsted three-button narrow-lapel italian-style (no seam up the back) jacket. The trousers are cut to 18" knee, 18" bottoms, no turnups. He looks at himself in the mirror while Toby, the cutter, hovers behind. He runs his finger along the left shoulder of the jacket. 'Look at this,' he says, 'a wrinkle.' Toby murmurs something about it smoothing out with wear. Bob loses his temper. 'With WEAR,' he shouts, 'three fucking fittings and thirty-five fucking guineas and you tell me it'll smooth out with WEAR! Take the fucking thing apart and do it again by next Saturday.' We have a coffee in the Wimpey Bar. Bob is still fuming. 'Cunt' he says, 'what does he take me for? Some fucking scruff?' We go down Charing Cross Road to Dobell's and buy some records. Micky goes to his alto sax lesson: Bob goes to see his bird. Colin and I take the train back to Welling. I arrange to call for him at eight that night – we've decided to go to the local dance hall, the Embassy, rather than back up to town. When I call for him he's still getting ready: ironing and starching two small white handkerchiefs into eight regular points for his top pocket (we scorn the pieces of stiff cardboard with neatly stitched triangles of cloth at the top that are becoming popular) and repolishing his new shoes. In the bar of the Rose and Crown we meet Brian and Micky, and Micky's brother Colin. Colin is about 5'4" (until this moment I'd not realised he had the same Christian name as Colin Medhurst), thirty years old, with a brown, almost bald, head.

This book is a book of distractions. I go to get a pack of cigarettes and my dark glasses. On the way out I start to read, for the first time, a notice on the wall:

WARNING

DO NOT TOUCH THIS EXTINGUISHER
Except When There is a Fire

———

TO OPERATE

1. Pull out pin on left side.
2. Point rubber at fire.
3. Squeeze handles together.

Through the kitchen window I see Raja Rao, who has been very sick for some days with asthma (it was he who answered the phone to you the other night) and a shape I realise must be his wife (as there is a strange blue car with New York plates outside the door). I look across the grass to Curt's house and a short tape flickers through, as it has been doing since sunday. The tape starts with a feeling of irritation at my ungraciousness in not taking a piece of Hortense's coffee cake at their housewarming on sunday afternoon. Then there's a counterpoint of a feeling of how ridiculous it is to even remember that, as I'm sure she didn't even notice. A low bass enters, composed of 'she made it herself' and 'they are both pleasant without being forced'. It ends with a chord which combines all these things and says 'you made a false move'. OK, Hortense, I'll have a piece of cake. Magnet runs over the tape. At night I can hear the loudspeakers from the Harness races.

Yesterday I sent Val a copy of Aram's book *Words & Photographs* for her birthday next tuesday, and I'll try to phone her. There's no tape I can play about her: she just changed the whole machine from mono to stereo.

I was talking about Micky's brother Colin. It was through him, early in the '50s, that I was cured of my middle-class view of the police. One saturday night, after a minor fight in the Drill Hall, Bexleyheath, I saw him arrested and put, unmarked, into a Black Maria. Next morning he appeared minus a tooth and with stitches across his head. 'Fell down the stairs to the cells.' And that trips a key back to Dudley standing outside his house in carefully arranged camouflage jacket and combat boots, calling for the police. And thinking that the world would be straight if he called them and shut his front door. Hasn't he heard about milk bottles and windows? Doesn't he know the revolution's not coming by mail? Enough. The University Album's not being played today.

He is dressed in a white gown and lies on a trolley being wheeled along a corridor: he is drowsy. Outside the operating theatre the trolley is stopped and a doctor in green overalls with a green face mask leans over and looks at him. He feels hands on his right arm, the chill of alcohol, the prick of a needle. A voice tells him to count backwards from ten. At once he feels wide awake, though his eyes are shut, and thinks 'this is taking a long time to work'. As he thinks 'work' he opens his eyes. There is an enormous weight on his chest. He is inside an oxygen tent. Eight hours have passed and the operation is over. He runs that thought through again: 'this is taking a long time to work'. He can see no break in it. He screams for them to take him out of the oxygen tent – the transparent plastic only a few inches from his face seems to be suffocating him. Two days later, when the nurse is out of the room, he forces himself out of bed and over to the table where, in a drawer, is his file. He reads how his heart was stopped, the blood pumped through a machine: how his breastbone was sawn in half, his heart stitched, his chest sewn up. He reads of the pints of blood poured into him and how, at the end of the operation, after his heart had been restarted, it stopped again, and how he'd been given massive shots of adrenalin to bring him back to life. Nowhere can he find the key.

I still run that thought through. Somewhere there must be a flaw in it. Somehow I must find the weak place, and snap it. It's too perfect to be human: it tastes of technology. When I wrote 'I feel like an android' I knew what I was writing.

Cancer was originally to have been published in 1973 by Harvey Brown's Frontier Press, designed and typeset by Holbrook Teter, with a drawing of a skull by Michael Myers on the front cover. Chronologically – in the order in which Tom Raworth wrote his books – it sits between *Moving* (1971) and *Pleasant Butter* (1972). This 2025 edition was prepared for Carcanet Press by Miles Champion on behalf of the Estate of Tom Raworth, using the original typescript dated 19/7/71 and marked 'final version' in the author's hand, and Michael Myers's original drawing, now held in the Zephyrus Image records, Special Collections, University of Delaware Library, Museums, and Press. 'Logbook' was first published, in very slightly altered form, as *Logbook* (Berkeley, CA: Poltroon Press, 1976); a revised version of 'Journal' was published as 'Notebook: January–March 1971' in *Acts*, no. 5 (1986); and a revised version of 'Letters from Yaddo' was published in *Visible Shivers* (Oakland, CA: O Books; Novato, CA: Trike, 1987). For timely assistance with the preparation of this volume some fifty years later, many thanks to Alastair Johnston, Olivia Teter and the Special Collections processing archivist at the University of Delaware Library, Dustin Frohlich.